You, your baby and play

At LEGO we're fascinated by the way good play helps people learn. Play teaches us about our world. It helps us explore fun ways to use both our bodies and our minds. And, perhaps most important in these changing times, play helps us better understand and get along with other people.

The arrival of your new baby is very special. It will be a wonderful time when both of you can simply have fun and play! Your baby has much to learn, and like many people involved in child development, we believe one of the best gifts you can give your baby is your love and attention through play.

That's why we've created this book, to show you *what* your baby is trying to learn through play and *how* you can create a good play environment in your home. It also introduces you to many of the play materials designed by LEGO to stimulate play and learning from the first days of your baby's life.

Throughout this book we have chosen to alternate the masculine and feminine pronouns "he" and "she".

I play to learn about...

you

One minute your baby is comfortably floating in the dark, snug and secure, relaxing to the rhythm of your heartbeat. The next minute she is suddenly thrust into our bright, noisy and odour-filled world. As your baby struggles to cope with this mix of new, exciting and threatening experiences, she reaches out, desperately seeking to be comforted so as to once again feel safe and secure.

Your baby reaches out for you.

And in the minutes, days, weeks and months that follow, between crying and sleeping, you'll start to play with your baby – and she'll love every minute. Why? Because she wants to learn about you, the person she trusts most, the person who can bring comfort no matter how scary this new world becomes.

Your baby is naturally curious and will become more aware of her surroundings with each passing day. In the earliest months, you can help her by singing and talking to her in playful voices and making funny faces. This will delight your baby (and bring a lot of joy to your heart as well).

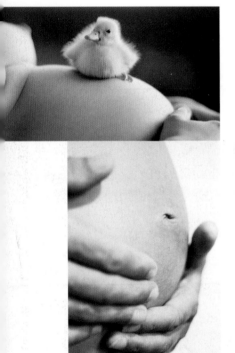

Your baby's brain is always working – even when she's fast asleep. The brain fills the upper half of the head, weighing about three pounds when fully developed. In addition to controlling many key body functions automatically, the brain is also home to your baby's emotions and feelings.

my body

You can easily get up and walk across the room. You can gracefully go up and down a staircase. You can peel a banana, snap your fingers or put a thread through the eye of a needle. And you can do all these things without really thinking about them.

Someday life will be this easy for your baby. But in the meantime, there's a lot he will need to learn about how to use this fascinating, hard-to-control and fast-growing bundle of head, body, arms and legs he suddenly finds himself living with.

Playing on his own, and during games you start, your baby will explore the power hidden in his body. He will learn how to use that power by trying new ideas and techniques (not always successfully and often with many tears). Through play you initiate, your baby will come to understand each part of his body and how different parts can be used together to make noises, to pick things up and let them drop, and, on one magical day, to lift himself up and start walking!

Your baby's ears help him hear and process the many sounds around him. They also help him keep his balance. Small, liquid-filled canals lined with thousands of microscopic hairs constantly sense all movements and relay balance information to the brain.

my
feelings

You don't cry when you're hungry or if your mother leaves the room. After all, you've learned to regulate your emotions. You are aware of your own feelings and sensitive to those of others. You care about other people and understand that they might think and feel differently than you do.

Your newborn is only aware of its own feelings. She has a difficult time coping with her emotions and can spend much time crying. But slowly your baby will become more aware of herself and more comfortable with, and curious about, the people and things that surround her. You'll notice that soon your baby will demonstrate increasing sensitivity and will cry when another child starts to cry, or become jealous if you pay attention to another child.

You can initiate playful situations that will help your baby understand her own feelings and those of others. For example, you might say how happy her doll is now that she's had some pretend food or how the doll is now sleeping. Also, when reading a book or watching something on television, you might point out how a character is feeling about the situation he or she faces.

Your baby's skin protects her internal organs from harm and keeps them at the temperature they prefer. Skin also gives her the ability to feel the world around her as millions of nerve endings continuously send messages to her brain telling her she feels hot or cold and whether she's experiencing pleasure or pain.

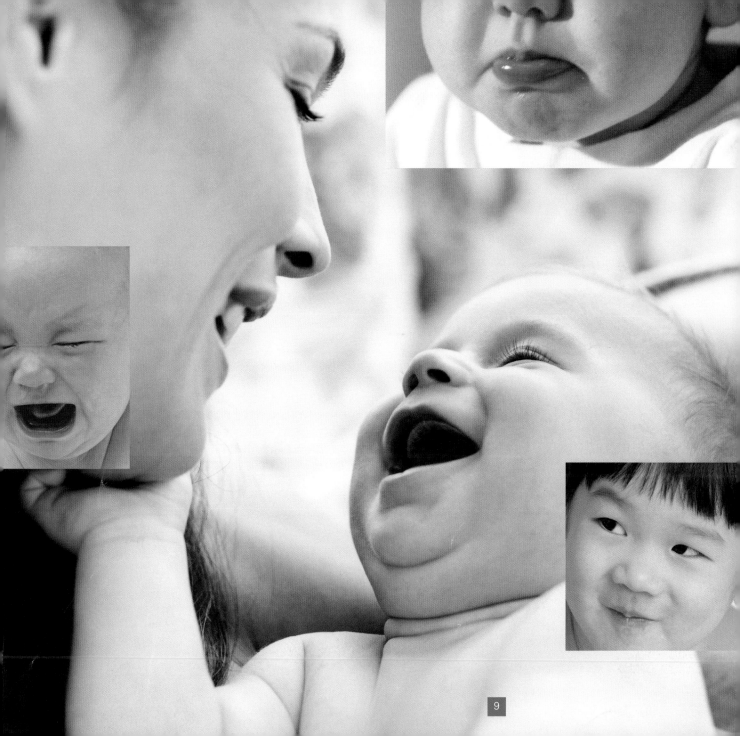

my
surroundings

You can be halfway down a familiar street before you realise where you are. You can walk from your bedroom to the bathroom in the dark. You can arrive at a party and quickly recognise the people you already know and those you haven't met (and you don't burst into tears when you meet a stranger who makes you feel uncomfortable).

For your newborn, there are no familiar sights, sounds, smells, tastes or textures. Everything is new... everyone is a stranger. But your baby is ready and eager to take in his new surroundings. From the earliest moments, your baby can see, hear, smell, taste and feel sensations. Like a sponge, your baby quickly absorbs his new world and starts collecting memories of the people (especially you), places and routines that surround him and bring him comfort.

You can use play to introduce your baby to his surroundings in a fun and non-threatening way. Play encourages and motivates your baby to cope with, and eventually master his world by helping him learn more and more about the people and things that are important to him.

Your baby uses his eyes to take in his surroundings. The image he sees appears upside down in the eye itself – the brain then takes the signal and turns it right side up. His eyes take care of themselves by using tears to remove unwanted germs and dust.

how things work

You know it is better to stack lighter objects on top of heavier ones. You know that water runs downhill. You know that yellow and blue make green. You know that ice is slippery, that glue is sticky and that ovens may be very, very hot. And if you don't know how or why something works the way it does, you know how to find out.

To your newborn, the mechanics of the world are a complete mystery. But as her thinking and physical skills develop, you'll find that her curiosity will drive her to constantly try to figure out (through often frustrating and tear-inducing experiments) how things work. Most important, you'll see how success in these endeavours will give her immense joy and ever-growing confidence.

You can use play to help your baby explore the physical world. Play provides a positive and challenging environment in which your baby can learn valuable lessons about the relationships between objects (for example, when she tries to put a square peg in a round hole), about the way our natural world works (for example, splashing in the bath) and how she can create (and avoid) events through her actions (for example, when she makes you appear and disappear as together you play peek-a-boo.

There are about 650 muscles in your baby's body; some that she needs to learn how to control and others that work automatically (such as the heart). Muscle makes up half your baby's body weight and each is made of hundreds, even thousands, of small fibres.

life

You know what makes you happy and content. You make friends with people who share your values. You co-exist in a society full of people who think, act and dress differently from you. You set goals – both short and long term – and you work hard to achieve them. You dream what some may call 'impossible' dreams.

It may seem like years before your baby will need the life skills necessary to be a successful adult. But the many experiences your baby will have in his first years will form the foundation upon which his adult experience will sit. The way in which he approaches life's challenges in the years to come will reflect the lessons you help him learn now, as a child.

Of course, play isn't the only way your baby will learn what he needs to survive and prosper in the adult world. But you'll find that play makes learning fun and attractive – for both you and your baby. Play will become more refined and complex as your baby grows. It will also become more challenging and rewarding the more capable, competent and confident he becomes.

No one knows how many seconds, minutes, hours or days your child will spend playing with you, or on his own, during his lifetime. But we do know that adults who were encouraged to spend considerable time playing as children are today happier and more contented than those who weren't encouraged to play. That's because in many ways play appears to build the foundation for the adult personality.

Essential play experiences

From birth to two years of age...

We've seen that your baby has much to learn and how learning through play will help her develop important life skills. Now we turn our attention to a series of landmark learning experiences that occur over the first two years of life.

Of course, every baby is unique and your baby may experience these landmarks a bit sooner or later than our age guides suggest. Use your best judgement and, if you do become concerned about your baby's development, please consult your paediatrician.

You will find it fun and rewarding using play to enhance your baby's natural curiosity and built-in desire to explore. As your baby grows, you will find yourself continuously amazed by the way she suddenly seems able to do new things. And you can take much of the credit for helping her to learn through play.

In the pages that follow, we share with you some learning experiences you may want to focus on at each of six stages in your baby's development from birth through to the age of two.

Experiencing colour

From birth...

As adults we know that red means 'stop' and green means 'go'. But your newborn is just getting accustomed to the idea of seeing colours for the first time!

At first your baby sees everything in black and white, but then bright, clear and contrasting colours such as red, yellow, blue and green start to be seen... and loved because they arouse his curiosity.

At first you can provide your baby with high contrasting colours like black and white. Then, after a few weeks, your baby will start to see colours! You can create a stimulating world in your home by selecting fun and colourful decorations and play materials. From time to time, treat your baby (and yourself) by placing an assortment of bright, fresh-cut flowers on the kitchen table.

Activity Friends
0-18 months

From birth...
Colourful, friendly faces produce bright smiles.

From about 3 months...
Your baby stretches and reaches for the hanging rings.

From about 6 months...
Separated rings and rattles can now be shaken, grasped and tasted.

From about 9 months...
The many pieces let you introduce numerous play situations to your baby.

Experiencing sound

From about 3 months...

Think of all the sounds you take in every day. Alarm clocks (recently replaced by your baby), telephones, running water, radios, televisions, vacuum cleaners, beeps at the supermarket checkout, planes crossing overhead, voices around the dinner table... the list goes on and on!

For your baby, this world of sound is fascinating, exciting and – when it's your soothing voice – most comforting. Before you know it, she learns how to make sounds by herself! It starts with her gurgles and the sucking sounds as she feeds.

Suddenly sound (you might call it noise) becomes more intentional through the vigorous shaking of her rattle that brings huge smiles of delight and satisfaction to her face. Patience please... she's learning through play! You can have fun with sound as well by making funny noises that amuse your baby. Your baby will also love to hear you talk about what you're doing around the house whether it's cooking meals, cleaning the house and giving her a bath.

MUSICAL APPLE
0-24 Months

From birth...
Soothing harmonic sounds comfort your baby making her feel safe and secure.

From about 3 months...
Happy faces and bright, contrasting colours stimulate and amuse your baby.

From about 6 months...
Your baby delights in making the Musical Apple rock back and forth.

From about 9 months...
You set the Musical Apple wobbling across the floor, your baby crawls after it.

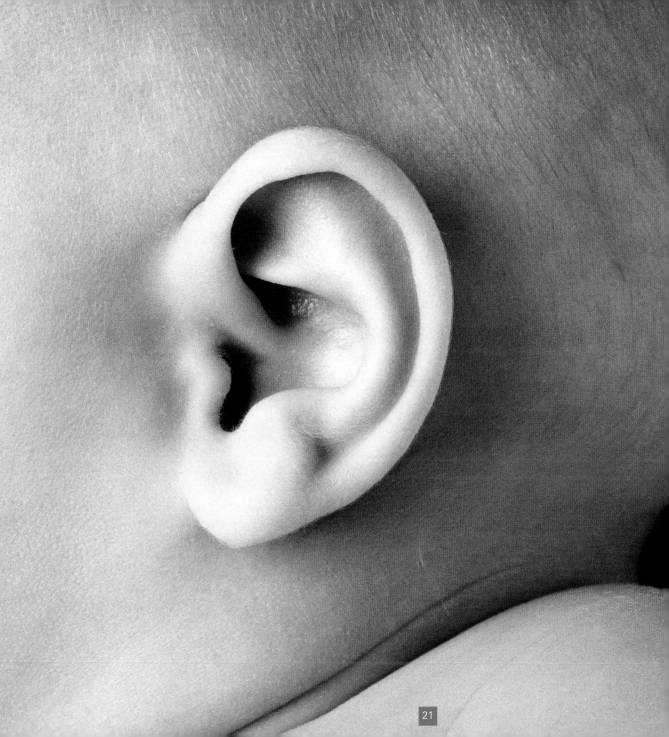

Experiencing
shapes and
textures

From about 6 months...

When you've finished reading this book, you'll probably place it on a shelf with a number of other books. What would your baby do?

In his earliest days, he will look curiously at the book's shape and feel its hard corners. His tender and sensitive hands will be smoothed. He will probably try to taste the book, and if it tastes good, he's likely to start chewing on it.

As he grows, he will behave more like you, and spend time putting things of the same shape together. He may develop a preference for certain shapes, and separate the 'round' or 'triangular' toys from all the rest. Make sure you expose your baby to as many shapes and textures as possible, both at home and outdoors (rocks, leaves, puddles, flowers, grass, sand, etc.).

My Rattle Friends
0-24 months

From birth...
Bright dots, stripes and happy faces stimulate your baby's curiosity.

From about 3 months...
Your baby enjoys grasping and holding the rattles.

From about 6 months...
Fun shapes and textures fascinate and stimulate your baby.

From about 9 months...
You use the two-sided rattle to play peek-a-boo with your baby.

Experiencing cause and effect

From about 9 months...

You know how to make things happen. For example, you put a tape in your video recorder, press a dozen or so buttons and relax knowing (or, at least, hoping) that your favourite programme will be taped even though your in-laws "dropped by".

But your baby has emerged from a world inside you in which everything just happened naturally. Quite quickly she has figured out that she can get your attention by crying, and from then on her fascination with making things happen grows day by day.

As your child grows you'll play the important role of initiating playful situations (often leaving your child to play on its own). For example, you may stack some blocks into a tower and then watch her knock the tower down with great satisfaction. This simple, yet important act shows she is setting goals and harnessing her motor skills to achieve them. It's also a way – at a time when so much of her life is controlled by others – of taking control of things. Success in these moments of play builds confidence and inspires your baby to go further faster.

Happy Explores Stack n' Learn.
6-24 months

From about 6 months...
Fun, cheerful blocks your baby can grasp, taste and toss about.

From about 9 months...
The rocking motion she can create fascinates your baby.

From about 12 months...
Making the catapult work again and again builds confidence.

From about 18 months...
You and your baby build a train and take the little figures for a ride.

Experiencing exploration

From about 12 months...

Do you remember what it feels like to visit a place for the first time; your first walk through a museum, for example, or your first day in a holiday resort? As you progress through these new spaces all of your senses are on full alert, taking in everything around you that is "new" and "different".

This is what your baby will experience as he becomes more and more aware of his surroundings. And once he starts moving on his own, first through crawling and then (get ready!) by walking, the world just keeps getting bigger and bigger! This is a time of great learning as your baby is exposed to more and more colours, shapes, textures, smells, sounds and language.

With only a few words with which to tell a story, your baby will use play to re-enact a simple event he has experienced (for example, feeding his teddy bear just the way he's been fed by you, by pushing a car along the floor just as he sees cars on his outings with mum or dad, or putting a stuffed animal to bed just as he has been tucked in by his mother). These re-enactments are the first 'stories' your child will tell. Your active participation will help him develop strong communication and emotional skills, since together you can explore some of the feelings in his story.

Playbook
6-36 months

From about 6 months...
Your baby starts to discover himself through the mirror.

From about 9 months...
You use the holes in which figures appear and disappear to play peek-a-boo.

From about 12 months...
Figures help your baby re-enact stories like taking a bath and playing with friends.

From about 18 months...
You use the book to help your baby learn new words, sounds and meanings.

26

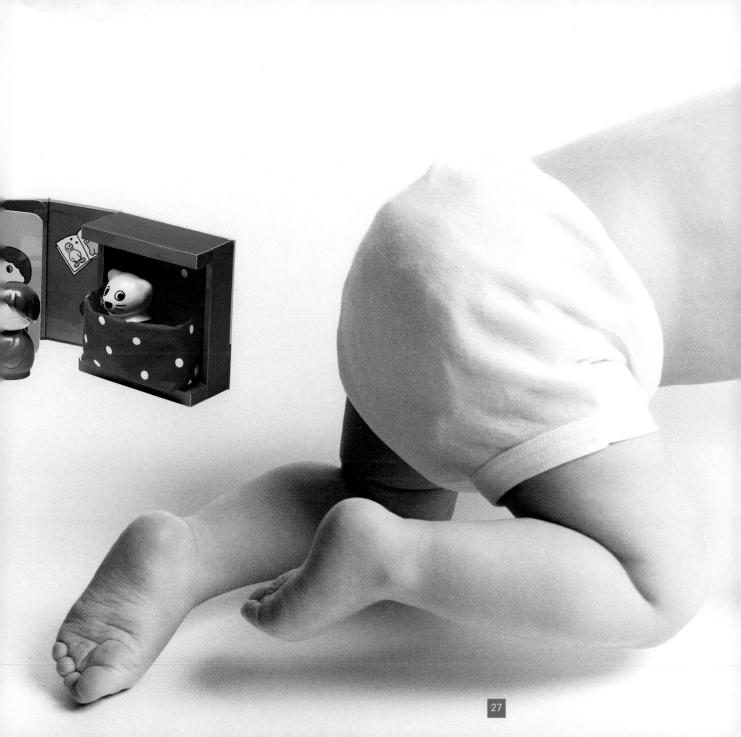

Experiencing problem solving

From about 18 months...

You can think of something you want or need to do and, before you know it, start taking the necessary steps to accomplish your task. You are able to draw upon a lifetime of experiences and easily put together a string of solutions that are needed to solve problems you face.

By the time your baby reaches about 18 months, she'll have spent many months accumulating skills through experimentation. This learning by trial and error starts to give way to new gestures and limited speech that indicates she's actually thinking about how she will solve problems she encounters.

You can stimulate this new-found problem solving capacity by introducing simple games and play situations that set simple challenges. You might also watch your child at play and congratulate her when you've noticed she's thought about something before acting.

Stack n' Sort
8-24 months

From about 8 months...
Your baby delights in opening and closing the door over and over again.

From about 12 months...
Blocks are combined in new ways and built into towers (that get knocked down!)

From about 18 months...
Your baby experiments to discover which shape fits into which hole.

28

Towards a richer parenting experience

For many people, there's no more powerful lifetime experience than bringing a child into the world. And despite all of the advances in science and technology that have uncovered many of the secrets of conception and life in the womb, most parents still use the word 'miracle' when describing the birth of their baby.

That's not surprising when we consider the result from the nine or so months of development from conception: a continuous division and reorganisation of cells that produce not only a living, breathing human body but also a totally unique individual with his own personality, fingerprints, and, of course, vocal chords.

We hope this book has given you a better insight into what your baby is trying to learn and how you can help your baby discover his potential and come to master his world by learning through play.

Have fun!